Leads To Referrals

Getting Rewarding Referrals From Your Contacts That Count!

Timothy M. Houston

www.leadstoreferrals.com

Edited by Martin J. Coffee

Coffee2Go Editing Services.
www.Elance.com/coffee2go

Cover Design by Ziziiryaspraha Subiyarta
Author Photo by Michelle Kawka
www.michellekawka.com

Houston-CB Group, Inc., publisher

Copyright © 2013 by Timothy M. Houston.
All rights reserved.

All trademarks or registered trademarks, logos and brand names and trade names used and referenced herein are property of their respective owners.

No part of this publication may be reproduced, stored in a retrieval system, or transmitted by any means, electronic, mechanical, photocopying, recording, scanning, or otherwise, except as permitted by Section 107 or 108 of the 1976 United States Copyright Act without the prior written permission of the copyright owner. Requests for permission or further information should be addressed to: Houston-CB, Group, Inc.at requests@leadstoreferrals.com

ISBN-13: 978-1467910521

Dedicated to Emily, Grandma Marie and the memory of my Grandpa Paul.

Each of you have touched and changed my life forever.

Note to the Reader
(a/k/a The Legal Stuff)

This publication contains the opinions and ideas of its author. It is intended to provide helpful and informative material on the subjects addressed. While the author and publisher have used their best efforts in preparing this book, the strategies outlined herein may not be suitable for every individual and are not guaranteed or warranted to produce any particular results. This publication is designed to provide accurate and authoritative information in regard to the subject matter covered. It is sold with the understanding that the author and publisher are not engaged in rendering legal, financial, accounting, or other professional services. The reader should consult with a competent professional before adopting any of the suggestions in this book or drawing any inferences from it.

No warranty is made with respect to the accuracy or completeness of the information referenced or contained herein and both the author and publisher specifically disclaim any implied warranties of merchantability or fitness for a particular purpose and further disclaims any responsibility for any liability, loss or risk, personal or otherwise, which is incurred as a consequence, directly or indirectly, of the use and application of any of the contents of this book. Neither the author nor publisher shall be held liable for loss of profit or any other commercial damages, including but not limited to special, incidental, consequential or other damages

Table of Contents

A Referral Reality Check	7
Stop Begging For and Start Earning Referrals	27
Great Referral Expectations	37
Who Are The People In Your (Referral) Neighborhood?	40
The Double-Triple Referral Reward	49
The Referral Raffle	58
From Competition to Collaboration	63
Let the Cause Become "The "Because"	70
The Big B.R.O. Event	81
Recognition Referrals	90
The Gateway to Referrals	100
The Referral Clinic	109
The Manilow Method	113
Your Hidden Referral Partners	120
I See, You See Referrals	137
Closed Loop Referrals	143
Now What?	153
Meet Tim Houston	156

Chapter 1

A Referral Reality Check

Old San Juan, Puerto Rico
September 18, 2009:

I was waiting patiently for him at my favorite restaurant in Old San Juan, Café Puerto Rico. I was already on my second café con leche when I got his phone call telling me he was running late but would be there "en cinco minutos"(in five minutes).

I had come to Puerto Rico to start a new venture with the help of several local business people; one of those people was Martin, an insurance broker who was referred to me by Janet, a client of mine in Orlando, Florida, after I had mentioned my new venture in Puerto Rico to her. In the two months that preceded my visit, we had a series of telephone and email conversations, and in one of our telephone conversations Martin made it a point to mention to me that *everyone* on the island knew him.

As I sat at my outdoor table, the streets of Old San Juan were filled with the locals as well as the tourists from the cruise ship that had docked earlier that morning. I was looking over Plaza Colon, listening to a group of local musicians performing for a crowd, when all of a sudden I saw a brand-new, blue Jaguar XKR convertible speed up and pull over alongside the restaurant and stop. The driver created his own spot in front of the restaurant, in spite of the traffic sign that read "No Estacione" (no parking).

Out of the car came a very well-dressed, middle-aged gentleman dressed in a silk suit, a gold wristband on his left arm, and a diamond encrusted Rolex watch on his right. Within seconds of him exiting the vehicle, people on the street started to wave and shout "¡Hola Martin!" (Even a passing police officer said hello and ignored the fact that he was illegally parked). Martin made his way over to my table. With a smile, the man who apparently needed no introduction extended his hand and introduced himself.

During our meeting, Martin explained to me that he had been in the insurance business for almost 15 years, starting off as an agent. In his first two years, he built a book of business that would have taken the average agent at least five years to do. By his fourth years in the business, he ventured out on his own and started his own insurance agency, which he built mostly through word-of-mouth marketing.

We spoke about my new business venture in Puerto Rico and he not only agreed to help introduce me to some of the island's movers-and-shakers, but he said he wanted to hire me as a consultant to help his business generate more referrals.

I was a little surprised to hear this. After all, everything about Martin exuded success -- from his brand-new, $90,000.00 car to his $25,000.00 Rolex watch and his $600 shoes.

"Tim, I have a large network of people. You can see for yourself that practically everyone on the island knows me. I'm involved with the Chamber of Commerce and so many organizations and charities. I have many clients who have been with me for over 10 years," he said.

"So what's the problem?" I asked inquisitively.

"It's a big problem: I'm not getting many referrals from these people."

"What do you mean?" I asked.

"They all believe that because I'm so successful that I don't *need* referrals. That's far from the truth. Now more than ever, I am competing against the big insurance companies with their millions of dollars in advertising and promotions that an independent agent like me can't compete against. For the past three years, about 20-25% of my clients have switched over to my competitors because of lower insurance rates," he said.

"And before you tell me that I need to ask my clients for referrals or do more networking, I've already done those things and that still doesn't produce enough results. I have been to the seminars; I have listened to the networking and word-of-mouth experts, read their books and have done with they have said and while I've grown my network, I need you to help me to find a solution that ***leads to referrals.***"

Referrals.

People love to get them. Businesses strive to increase their numbers. Most business owners and experts liken referrals to the "holy grail" when it comes to building their business, increasing awareness of their brands, and as a testament to client loyalty.

For almost 20 years, I have had the privilege or working with thousands of business people from around the world to make their businesses more productive, profitable, and prosperous. Whether it was working with solo entrepreneurs or Fortune 500 companies, every single one of them believed that referrals helped to grow their business.

Whether I'm consulting with a client or speaking before an audience at a seminar, I always ask the same question: Why do they like referrals? Very often I receive the following answers:

"They represent a person's trust and confidence in you."

"Referrals are easier to close."

"Referrals provide a greater ROI."

"Referrals are usually pre-qualified for your product/service."

"Referrals cost nothing compared to other forms of advertising."

"Referrals are an endorsement of you, your business, and its products/services."

So it's no surprise that business people want more referrals. But whenever I ask how do they get referrals, 90% of the time people will say it's mostly because of "Word-of-Mouth."

The Power of Word-Of-Mouth

Business people have a fundamental belief that positive Word-Of-Mouth (WOM) will often lead to referrals. Every year, research and studies continuously show how powerful WOM actually is:

- In 2012, Nielsen reported that 92% of consumers trust the recommendation of someone they know when it comes to a product or service versus all other forms of advertising (Print, radio, digital, and TV).[1]
- 59% of Americans believe that offline (face-to-face or voice-to-voice) word-of-mouth to be highly credible. (Source: Word of Mouth Marketing Association, 2011)

---

[1] Trust in Advertising. Retrieved January 30, 2013. http://blog.nielsen.com/nielsenwire/nielsen-news/trust-in-advertising-%e2%80%93-paid-owned-and-earned/

- Harris Poll Interactive found that 79% of people who had a memorable product purchase, use, or service experience will take action afterward and 57% of them will communicate positively about it with others, mostly offline.
- Mintel found that people still prefer to give real-life referrals rather than online, finding that most people who bought a product or service based off a recommendation did so on a referral from a friend/relative or husband/wife/partner (34% and 25%, respectively).[2]

So in order to get more referrals, most business people will engage in those activities that they believe will generate WOM and result in referrals. People will focus their efforts on generating more WOM through networking with others. Some go to their local Chamber of

---

[2] http://www.mintel.com/press-centre/press-releases/358/mintel-finds-people-still-prefer-real-life-recommendations-to-online

Commerce's business-after-hours programs and participate in social networking sites like LinkedIn and Facebook in the hopes of meeting new people and deepening existing relationships to the point where they will become referral sources. They ask their current clients for referrals, believing that since the client has already done business with them, it's "natural" for them to refer others who also need their product/service....

...but then it happens.

This Big Disappointment:

All too often, the end result of these activities is that most business people, like my client Martin, become *relationship rich and yet remain referral poor.*

Businesses don't understand that even if there is a positive buzz about their business in the business community, even if there are thousands or millions of "likes" on their Facebook page or if they have thousands of Twitter followers or connections on LinkedIn, if they fail (or do not know how) to consistently stimulate, motivate, teach, nurture, and transform their clients, their existing referral sources, and the new relationships they have built into generators of rewarding referrals, their business will not prosper.

Consider the following:

- In 2010, a study called *The Economics of Loyalty* conducted by Advisor Impact, Charles Schwab Advisor Services, and researchers at Texas Tech found that most satisfied clients **do not** refer new potential clients. In fact, the study revealed that while 91% of satisfied clients would be "somewhat or very comfortable providing a referral" **only 29% of them actually do!**

- As reported in *Business Networking AND SEX (not what you think)* (Entrepreneur Press, 2012), an international survey of over 12,000 business people found that 50.5% of women and 49.5% of men found that their greatest weakness in networking was "being unable to turn relationships into business opportunities."
- In the same Harris Poll cited earlier, while 52% of people will communicate positively about their experience in purchasing a product or use of a service, only 41% of people will actually recommend/refer people to buy the product/service. (What's not determined in this study is the final result of the actual referrals, [i.e., are they converted into paying clients]?).

- A *Harvard Business Review* study found that out of 9,900 customers surveyed at a telecom provider, while 81% of the customers said they would refer the company, only 30% actually did. Of those new referrals, very few generated actual customers: only 12% became customers, of which only 8% were ***profitable new customers***. Similar results were found with a financial firm's 6,700 clients: 68% said they would refer, only 33% did; 14% of the referrals turned into clients, with a mere 11% becoming profitable new customers. (Source: How Valuable Is Word of Mouth?, *HBR*, October 2007)

WOM & Referrals: A Land of Confusion

Most people are confused as they tend to equate Word-of-Mouth Marketing (WOMM) and the referral marketing and generation process as one in the same. There are hundreds, if not thousands, of books, articles, videos, training courses, programs, seminars, and scholarly research from many experts, some professors, authors, and trainers who (knowingly or unknowingly) combined the two concepts together many years ago and used WOMM and referral marketing/generation interchangeably. This has caused a saturated market of ideas which merely rephrases or repeats what most of these industry leaders say. (Just go to Amazon.com or Google and search for the terms "referrals" and "word-of-mouth and you'll see what I mean).

The problem is that there has been an evolution – perhaps a revolution – that goes largely unnoticed by most people. The truth is that Word-Of-Mouth Marketing and Referral Marketing/Generation are not the same, and the confusion is actually costing people business.

WOMM and referral marketing/generation are two different yet interdependent processes which need to be understood.

WOMM is a passive activity, the effects of which can become viral if cultivated and developed correctly. WOMM relies on others to spread the word about your products/service. You can't fully control it, but you can take steps to generate it and (in the case of negative WOMM) mitigate the negative results. For example, networking amplifies your WOMM campaign. It allows you build new relationships and enhance existing ones to get the word out on the street and also reinforces your business to those who may already know you and/or are doing business with you.

Positive WOMM is about getting people to spread great stories about their experiences with your products/services. When they do, then it creates the opportunity to generate new business referrals through your referral marketing/generation strategies.

Referral marketing/generation is active. It is geared toward those people who have an interest, want, need, or desire for your product/service and are receptive to communicating and interacting with you. Generating, cultivating, and using positive WOM that is geared towards you, your products, or services is just one factor in generating new, qualified referrals.

Once you have the positive WOM, you need to have a referral generating system in place that motivates, stimulates, and causes people to refer others to you. Unlike WOMM, a referral marketing and generating system is predictable, controllable, and focuses on the desired end result.

But Are You Referable?

Bill Cates, author of *Get More Referrals Now* (McGraw-Hill, 2004), says that you know you are referable when you are getting referrals without asking for them. While that is true to some extent, especially for those who have become, as my friend Bob Burg says in his book *Endless Referrals* (McGraw-Hill, 2005), "the expert (and only logical resource) in [their] field," it's just one metric of the referral process. In today's super-crazy, overworked, attention-deficit world, most people need to be reminded and aware of who you are, what you do, what you offer, and why they should do business with and refer business to you.

Being referable is more than just doing a good job for someone and then hoping/expecting that they will refer others with whom they have relationships to you, in the event those people need your services/products.

It's more than just meeting new people and growing the size of your network. Networking is critical and needs to be done in any business, but it's about transforming and leveraging your contacts that count into relationships that generate rewarding referrals.

It's more than people just "liking" you and your company online. Just because someone "likes" you doesn't mean they will do business with you or refer you. You have to connect and engage with people in the real world as well. As John More, COOP (that's *Chief Operating Officer Person*) of Brains on Fire, an identity company in Greenville, South Carolina and the co-author of *The Passion Conversation* (Wiley, 2013), says: "The LIKE button will become much more UNLIKEABLE as more businesses focus on ways to connect with people in the physical world and not the digital world."

As I explained to Martin, being referable today is about being proactive in keeping people aware about who you are and what you do.

It's about getting them motivated to take action through incentives to provide you with qualified referrals – people who want, need, or desire your services or products.

It's about rewarding and recognizing your sources in ways that they appreciate (and in most cases that doesn't mean money!).

It's about making it easier for them to refer you with the utmost confidence. Don't make them jump through hoops or go through great lengths to refer you.

It's about making *them* look and feel good about their decision to refer you to those within their various networks.

This book is not about networking or WOM *per se.* This is not about converting sales leads to referrals. It is about implementing simple and effective referral marketing and generating strategies, tactics, and techniques to captivate, motivate, activate, nurture, reward, and retain those people in your various networks to provide you with qualified referrals.

While some tactics and techniques in this book may seem obvious to you, some others might not. Some may seem brand-new, while you may have heard about others before but there is a new spin or enhancement. What makes this system work is that it is a proactive, predictable, scalable system – one that has been tested and implemented time and again by business people in different industries, with different levels of experience – from start-ups to seasoned businesses people, like Martin.

You don't have to implement everything to see an increase in referrals to your business. Pick and choose the strategies that appeal to you and put them into action, then share your results with me on www.leadstoreferrals.com.

Whether you want just a few more referrals or want to transform your business into doing business exclusively by referral only, the strategies and techniques in *Leads To Referrals* are designed to produce maximum returns for your referral efforts so that business will become more productive, profitable, and prosperous.

Did You Know...

According to the Online Etymology Dictionary, the word "referral" was first used between 1920 and 1935[3] and is defined as "the act of referring. From refer." By 1955, the sense of the word was that the act of referring was "especially to an expert or specialist."

---

[3] referral. (n.d.). *Online Etymology Dictionary*. Retrieved January 30, 2013, from Dictionary.com website: http://dictionary.reference.com/browse/referral

Chapter 2

Stop Begging For and Start Earning Referrals

> *"Never stand begging for that which you have the power to earn."*
>
> – Miguel de Cervantes

Each year, I attend hundreds of networking events, seminars, business expos, and trade shows. I often find that 20-25% of the business cards I receive contain the following phrase, usually on the reverse side: "The biggest compliment you can give me is a referral…" usually followed by something like "to your friends/family/colleagues or someone who could use my product/service."

While a phrase like this may seem harmless to most people, it causes me to cringe.

Here's why it doesn't work well

Reality #1: Having a phrase like this on your business card, website, social media profile, or email signature lines is a sign of desperation. To a seasoned networker and businessperson, it gives the impression that the person is begging for referrals.

Reality #2: It also presumes that the receiver of the card wants to give you referrals.

To put it bluntly, the people who just met you *don't care about YOU at this point.*

You may be the greatest person in your profession, but until you start, develop, and nurture a relationship with them, they will not want to take a risk on referring someone to you; they are not going to put their reputation on the line by providing a referral to you because you haven't earned their trust…yet.

Reality #3: Those who do know, like, trust, admire, and respect you will refer people to you only when *they* are confident in your ability to a) provide a valuable, positive experience to the person being referred (i.e., the prospect), and b) you make them (i.e., the Source) look great in the eyes of the prospect. The prospect always wants reassurance that the Source is "doing the right thing." Likewise, the Source has more to lose than the Receiver has to gain: their personal and professional reputation as well as their relationship with the prospect. There could also be a significant financial risk on their end based upon your performance.

Sometimes begging is disguised as "asking" for referrals. For decades, sales trainers would teach a rather annoying "technique" as part of a basic sales training course: that you should ask everyone within three feet of you and especially those with whom you've done business with, if they could provide the names and contact information of three people who they think could benefit from your product/service. Then the salesperson would call or otherwise solicit those people and tell them that they were referred to you by the person who gave you their names.

In short, this is nothing but a cold call and to this day it is still being taught by many sales training companies and remains a standard operating procedure used by many of those in the insurance and financial industries. (My colleague Andy Lopata, author of ***Recommended: How to sell through Networking and Referrals*** calls this "a lead generation strategy (at best) that is impatient, poorly timed and is lazy.") In fact in an article about referrals and the wealth-management industry, *The Wall Street Journal* reported:

> "Wealth-management practices are built by word of mouth. Consultants are full of ideas for how advisers can win new-business referrals from clients. Most of this advice comes down to asking clients straight out for help. Proponents say these nudges work because most clients are willing to refer their advisers to friends and family--83% of them, according to Pershing LLC--but just 4% take action on their own.
>
> On the other hand, it isn't hard to find

advisers who dislike this approach. They know most new business comes from referrals--66%, says a study by Moss Adams and InvestmentNews. Yet advisers prefer to earn them unasked than make direct pitches for them."[4]

So how do you stop begging for referrals and start actually earning them? You need to position yourself to your referral sources and your current clients as providing exceptional value and experiences in everything you do. This can be done in a variety of different ways beyond just doing what the client is paying you for or by providing your referral sources with what they're looking for.

Here are two simple strategies that can earn you more referrals (and bigger profits) for your business:

---

[4] Coyle, T. (2012, November 2). Asking for Referrals Outright Can Make Clients Squirm. *The Wall Street Journal*. Retrieved from :
http://online.wsj.com/article/SB10001424052970203707604578094820819867116.html#articleTabs%3Darticle

Give your best clients "Preferred Status"

Everyone wants to be treated "special." Credit card companies have platinum cards for their "best" cardholders; theaters and hotels have VIP sections which offer something extra special to those who have reached a certain level or purchase a certain ticket or package. When it comes to referrals, you have earned the trust and the business of your current clients, now it's time to leverage it.

Take a look at your current clients/customers/patients, identify your "best" clients, and let them know that you will provide them with an incentive, such as special pricing or some sort of extra bonus, if they refer a new, qualified client to you that meets your specific criteria.

For example, one of my clients, a day spa, sent a personalized letter (yes a *real* letter, not an email) to their top 23 clients who have purchased a minimum number of packages or spa services (5 packages totaling over $1,500) in the past year. In the letter, they told this group of clients that they are just one of a specific number of clients (in this case, 23) who have reached "preferred status." As a preferred customer, they can obtain a one-time-only, specially designed spa package valued at $500.00 for free if they refer 3 new clients that make 2 purchases in the next 3 months that total at least $400.00. The letter contained a special code which identifies the referral source which the prospect gives at the time of their reservation.

The special spa package given to the referral source cost the spa $250.00. If just one customer sends three referrals to the spa and each buy services totaling $200.00 in month #1, the spa now has $600.00 in initial sales. When the three referrals come back the following month, they spend another $200.00 each. The source of the referrals (the preferred client) has earned their special spa package which they can book at any time during the next 6 months to a year.

The spa invested $250.00 in the referral source and made $950.00 in sales from these three referred clients provided by just one of their "preferred clients." Using this example, if 10 of their "preferred clients" refer 3 people each, they will net $28,500.00 in sales after an investment of only $2,500.00. The referrals now turn into clients who continue to use the spa's services and who could refer others. The original source of these new customers continues to rave about the spa and keeps their "preferred" status.

The Privilege of Priority Access

Why do people pay more money to fly first class on an airline? Why do people spend hundreds of dollars each year in fees to have a certain credit card that offers perks like opportunities to purchase tickets to a concert or event before they go on sale to the general public? One of the biggest reasons is that they want what I call the "Privilege of Priority Access." This technique works well with referral sources and clients alike.

You can go to your best clients and referral sources and let them know that before you take on any new clients/customers from the outside, you want to offer them the opportunity to refer new, qualified prospects to you within a short period of time. When they refer a qualified prospect, you will consider their referral as a new client/customer *before* anyone else. If the prospect becomes a client, both the prospect and the referral source will have access to any new products/services you offer *before* the rest of the public does, for up to one year.

If you are a service provider, like an attorney or CPA, you could give these clients and referral sources a special phone number or email address where they could access you directly. You could also offer them a complimentary hour-long consultation or review, once a quarter. If you are part of a larger practice and if you are in a good financial position to do so, you can have your associates work with new clients/patients who come from your advertising efforts while you only work with those who were referred by your existing clients.

You have the ability to customize the experience based upon your profession. It's all about being creative enough to make them think of you more often and talk about you more often than your competitors.

Remember: While asking for a referral is fine begging for one isn't. Instead of asking everyone you meet for a referral, determine who the people are in your networks that have already provided exceptional value to you. Then continuously provide exceptional value for them, and you'll earn their referrals every time.

Chapter 3

Great Referral Expectations

A colleague of mine was lamenting over a situation she found herself in. She told me that she had a new client that took up a tremendous amount of her time and that of her staff. The client was at times extremely belligerent and very demanding, to the point where each interaction consumed most of my colleague's energy and her day.

I asked why she was continuing to work with this particular client. She replied that it was a referral from a very good friend who was also a major source of business referrals. Fearing that she would hurt her feelings or insult her friend, she decided to "grin and bear it."

As the story unfolded, it turned out that the source of the referral "oversold" the prospect on my colleague's company's services and abilities. The prospect was left to believe that my colleague's company could do almost anything, in record time, and that they would be at the prospect's beck and call. This created a very uncomfortable situation for my colleague until the project was completed.

Over the years, much has been written about the importance of exceeding your customer's expectations. While this is incredibly important in business when it comes to referral generation, you must first manage the expectations of your potential client by educating the source of the referral, first.

For example, your referral source may be so excited to give a referral to you that they overstate your abilities and availability. On other occasions, the source may tell the prospect that you have the "lowest price" while that may not be the case. Because they are being referred by someone who they know and trust, sometimes the prospect automatically expects a discount or some other kind of special service or perks. In most cases, this will happen because of the source's overstatements before they even gave you the referral and always because of a lack of understanding between you and the referral source.

Since the prospect was referred to you, the source must always communicate accurate information about you and your business to those they will be referring. You need to tell your source exactly how they should promote you, what to say, and how to say it to a prospect, before they even speak to the prospect. You also need to tell them what you will say and do for that prospect when they communicate or meet with you after the referral is made. That way, there are little or no misunderstandings and the expectations are set between the three people involved.

Don't leave it up to the referral source to figure it out or, even worse, leave it up to chance. By teaching your source what to say, how to say it, and what you will do for the prospect, it will make it easier for you to manage, meet and exceed everyone's expectations and lead to future referrals.

Chapter 4

Who Are The People In Your (Referral) Neighborhood?

Growing up, I loved Sesame Street. One of my favorite songs sung by Bob McGrath was called "Who Are the People in Your Neighborhood?" This great, catchy song always featured Bob in a segment with a Muppet that depicted someone in a profession that you would commonly see in your neighborhood. The purpose of this segment of the show was to teach children a little bit about what these people did on a daily basis. They would ordinarily showcase blue collar, white collar, and eventually, "no collar" professions on each show.

While most of us are quick to say that we know who these people are and what they do, quite often these people are just "in the background" of our lives. Sure they are there, but we tune them out unless we need them for our own reasons. I believe that once we do this, we limit ourselves and close our ability to network effectively, let alone develop referrals.

Here are five examples of people in our "networking neighborhood" that we may encounter on a regular basis and yet never think of as referral sources:

A waiter/waitress

They do more than just take your orders and deliver the food. In almost every coffee shop, diner, or upscale restaurant, there will always be a wait staff member that people love to have. No matter when you go, they make the experience worthwhile. Quite often, these people seem to know EVERYONE in the community. Over the years, I have met people who have gotten some great referrals from wait staff members or who received introductions by these people to others they never thought they would be able to meet.

Here's a technique that I found to work well and generate referrals for me: If you're a "regular" at a particular restaurant and have a favorite server, let them know what you do for a living and offer three of your business cards when you pay the bill. Tell your server that one is for their reference and ask them to give out the other two. At a particular diner I frequent, I have gotten to know three waitresses over a 10 year period. Each of them have referred almost 30 qualified, paying clients during this time. Even though that averages about 3 referrals per year, it didn't cost me anything more than my meals and further strengthened my relationships with them. I have shown my appreciation not only through tips ranging in the 50% range, but also providing them with thank-you gifts ranging from gift cards to concert tickets.

The barber or hairstylist

Going to the barbershop or hair salon is more than just a hair-cutting experience for many people. People will talk about things ranging from politics to social issues to the latest gossip. It's also a therapeutic session for others, (and often less expensive then psychotherapy). People will travel miles to go to a great barber or stylist, even if the barber or stylist leaves their current place of business. A savvy networker knows that the hairstylist or barber is usually both a great referral source and a gatekeeper to hundreds of people in the community and is worth getting to know in between haircuts and highlights.

The mailperson or delivery person

In most countries, businesses have their mail delivered before residential customers. Private delivery services like UPS or FedEx usually are used by more businesses than private individuals and they offer pick-up services at a place of business. Both the mailperson and delivery person usually have set routes that they follow and they tend to know business people or their staffs fairly well. By cultivating relationships with these delivery or mail people, you can develop trust and elicit referrals or introductions from them.

The local firefighters

Whether you live in a town with a volunteer fire department or a local firehouse in big city neighborhood, it seems that everyone knows who their firemen (or firewomen for those of you who have them) are. When they are not fighting fires, they can be found shopping in the local markets for food; perhaps they demonstrate fire safety tips in schools or for local civic groups.

But what people don't realize is that sometimes, some of these firemen are also entrepreneurs running businesses on the side. I met a network marketer who built more than half of her down-line by targeting volunteer fireman and rescue workers in her state. Her strategy was that because they have the extra time plus the credibility in the community, they were a natural target market to not only use her products but also to become distributors. (You don't have to be in network marketing to use a similar strategy to acquire referrals or to be introduced to key people.) A chiropractor who recently opened his practice in a new community asked the members of his referral group for referrals to first responders who lived/worked in that community. He offered free examinations and adjustments on their first visit. The result was that he received 32 referrals within three months' time. Eleven of those referrals generated an average of *three referrals each* over the year, providing a total of 33 new paying patients who were not first responders and billable income in excess of $75,000.00.

Teachers and principals of schools

If you have kids (or ever were one), you know that everyone in the community knows who the teachers are in a particular school. Chances are you also know who the principal and assistant principals are as well. Many of these professionals are tenured (at least in the United States), and many will spend years – in some cases decades – at the same school. Some of these teachers will participate in extracurricular activities as a sports team coach or advisor to an academic team. Others may spend their non-school time and summer vacations tutoring students. It's not uncommon for business people to partner with local schools to help the school and its students to achieve certain goals or to raise money for teams. These provide awesome opportunities to obtain and provide referrals.

A networking group in Brooklyn, New York decided to "adopt" a public middle school in their local area. The invited the principal, some guidance counselors, students, and even the officers of the Parent-Teacher Association to one of their chapter meetings. The result was that many of the group's members were asked to speak at the school's "Career Day" later that semester.

The podiatrist in the group was approached by one teacher after his presentation. She had a condition that was making it very difficult for her to walk and which ultimately required surgery. It worked out well for the teacher because she got the care she needed and was able to walk without being in agonizing pain; it worked well for the podiatrist because he earned over $5,000.00 for the surgery and received additional referrals of parents and other teachers due to the positive word-of-mouth that the teacher provided to him – all because the podiatrist spoke at a Career Day.

Your neighborhood is a great place to generate referrals, especially with (as the song from Sesame Street goes):"the people that you meet, when you're walking down the street, they're the people that you meet.......each day!"

YOUR NEXT STEPS:

1. Identify three people in professions that you see each day but never really considered to be potential referral sources.

2. Once you identify them, provide them with an opportunity to either experience your product/service for free or at a reduced rate. If they don't have an immediate need, extend the offer to whenever they need it or, as an alternative, to one of their friends/family members. If a family member/friend was referred to you, that person must tell you that they were referred by "Bob the mailman" or "Mrs. Carson, the first grade school teacher" in order to get the discount or free service/product.

3. Make sure you thank the person for thinking of you and for taking you up on the offer. Remember to ask how you may be able to help them in return.

4. If there's a person in the community that you want an introduction to that they may know, you need to ask them. Even if they do not know the person well enough, they may know someone within that person's company/organization who can facilitate the introduction for you.

Chapter 5

The Double-Triple Referral Reward

"You don't reward reaction, you reward results."

-- Edwin Louis Cole

This one seems *so* easy that most people are doubtful that it can work for their business. It is designed to produce a steady stream of new referrals, while at the same time generating more sales from existing clients. I have found that it can work in almost any profession and works extremely well with industries that have regular, recurring clients.

How it works:

1. You announce to all of your current clients that you truly appreciate their trust and

confidence in you. You are honored whenever they refer a family member, a friend, or neighbor to you. You explain that when they refer people to you it's more than just a compliment, but also serves as an affirmation that your clients are getting the best experience and benefits you and your service/products offer.

2. As a show of thanks, whenever someone they refer becomes your client, the referral source is offered two choices: something outside of your business that is valued at a certain dollar amount *or* they can have something *offered by you* worth **two or three times** the value of the initial reward offered.

Why it works:

1. The availability of an attractive, instant reward can be made to stimulate the referral source to a) think about your business and b) cause them to act towards getting something that *they* want and can use now or to receive a particular, valuable benefit, later.

2. The choices are limited to two rewards versus just one or dozens. This gives the referral sources a feeling of control because they are able to choose which reward to receive. Too many referral programs give either one reward or too many choices.

Research has shown that the more options that are available to a person, the less they are able to choose or they choose to take no action whatsoever. (For more examples and some groundbreaking research, including the "jam study" read *The Art of Choosing* [Twelve, 2013] by prominent social psychologist and professor at Columbia University, Sheena Iyengar.)

3. If people choose the lower, "outside" reward, then there is a fixed amount of your investment in your referral source and it's very easy to predict your profit from the referral. If they chose the double/triple reward, chances are that the referral source will buy more from you than the actual value of the reward. This not only results in additional profits, it reinforces client loyalty from

your referral sources which, in turn, could result in more referrals from them.

Here are some examples of how this system has been successfully implemented:

Dentist: Chad is a dentist in Washington who was looking to increase the amount of referrals from his existing patients. He started a referral program that allowed them to choose either a $25 gift card of their choice or receive a $50 credit towards a future dental service whenever they referred a new patient. Not only did he internally market this to his patient-base, he also sent out press releases announcing this new referral program. The story was picked up by the local media and the resulting publicity helped to further distinguish Chad from his competition.

Travel Agent: Nancy specializes in cruise vacations. Knowing that about 35% of all cruises are booked each year because of word-of-mouth referrals and that 60% of all cruisers are repeat clients,[5] she introduced a referral program available to those of her repeat clients who booked a cruise within the last two years.

If they referred a friend who booked a 7-day (or more) cruise, they would receive either a $100.00 cruise credit to be used onboard their next cruise if taken within the next year (in addition to any promotional credit offered by the cruise line), or $200 off a future cruise booking through her agency, which could be used anytime on any cruise line within the next two years.

Over the course of a year, Nancy booked an additional 41 cruises during the year, with an average cruise booking price of $1,700 per person.

Using this program, she averaged four new referrals per month. The majority of the referral sources who selected the $100 onboard credit reward were those who were already booked on a cruise and were sailing within the next six to ten months.

---

[5] Source: Florida-Caribbean Cruise Association 2012 Cruise Industry Overview. Retrieved from http://www.f-cca.com/downloads/2012-Cruise-Industry-Overview-Statistics.pdf

Here's a great case of the double-trip referral reward with a slight twist:

Auto Mechanic: Jerry owned a very successful auto service and repair shop. Most of his clients live or work within a 10-mile radius of his shop. He offers a seasonal maintenance package every summer and winter and wanted to increase the amount of new people purchasing his summer maintenance packages, which started at $120.00.

Jerry entered into an agreement with a very popular local restaurant that had an average wait time of about 25 to 30 minutes, and the average dinner for two at this restaurant was about $60, excluding taxes and gratuities. Jerry agreed to purchase a minimum of 20 of their gift cards per month, for three months, valued at $30 each -- a total value of $1,800. Because he bought repeatedly in volume, he negotiated a discount of $5.00 on each card; so each card was valued at $30, but he paid $25 them. His total investment over three months was $1,500.00.

He then sent his client mailing list of 2,200 people a postcard and then a follow-up letter which announced that for every new client they referred who bought a summer maintenance package, the referral source could choose between the $30 gift card to the restaurant or they could receive a $90 credit toward their next auto servicing or repairs, which could be used anytime in the next six months. (He also promoted this referral program in his shop so new "drive-in" clients could participate as well.)

Here's the twist which helped to make this offer so appealing: For about the cost of $5 per month plus the cost of calls, Jerry had a special toll-free number which was given to his clients that opted to receive the restaurant gift card. This dedicated number would allow them to make a reservation with the restaurant within 30 minutes of their arrival time.

At the end of the referral program, 127 new clients were referred to Jerry. Jerry gave out sixty-nine $30 restaurant gift cards to his referral sources (remember, he bought these at $25, so his investment was $1,725.00). He gave thirty-eight

$90 credits which could be used over the next six months at his shop, (total potential investment of $3,420.00). His total investment in this referral program was $5,145.00, excluding the toll-free number ($5 per month, plus the calls, which averaged about $15 per month).

Based on the average sale of $120 for the maintenance package, his 127 new clients generated an average of $15,240.00 in new sales with an average profit of $10,095.00.

(In reality, Jerry's actual profit was greater, as these figures do not take into account any of the extra repairs that some of the new clients purchased in addition to the summer maintenance package, the various referral sources who did not use the $90 credit during the six-month redemption period, or those referral sources who referred more than one person and yet only received one of the rewards.)

The Double-Triple Referral Reward is a small investment that pays off huge returns. It is scalable to almost any industry and provides you with a way to generate more referrals and sales from your existing clients. It can increase their motivation to refer business to you while truly rewarding people for the results they produce.

Try it for three months and share your results with me on www.leadstoreferrals.com.

Chapter 6

The Referral Raffle

Raffles are usually associated with fund-raisers for charities, non-profit organizations, and community groups. They can also generate new referrals for your business by giving your existing clients an opportunity to win something of value. They are also very simple to implement regardless of whether your business sells to consumers or to other businesses.

How it Works:

Unlike games of chance, which require one to purchase tickets with money, those who want to participate in The Referral Raffle earn an entry for each person they refer to you who becomes a paying client. It is also very flexible in terms of entry requirements. For example, you can establish a minimum number of referrals needed in order to earn an entry. The prize offered needs to be of a significant perceived value in order to attract and motivate people to refer to you. Although you can hold a Referral Raffle on a monthly basis, I have found it to work well when used no more than twice a year, as it creates motivation and activity on the part of your current clients to refer people to you in order to earn an entry.

A word of caution: before implementing a Referral Raffle, check with your attorneys and/or tax advisors as some countries and some state governments may deem raffles of any kind to be gambling and it could be illegal or there can be significant tax implications for you and the winner.

The Relaxation Referral Raffle

Rhonda is a licensed massage therapist in New York City. Rhonda's massages were geared towards stress relief as well as medical massage services which helped people to recover from musculoskeletal injuries. Rhonda retained my services to help her to increase the number of referrals from her current clients. I asked Rhonda what most of her clients say about their experience at her massage studio. She had about a year's worth of feedback/comment cards from her clients and one general theme was persistent: they all felt "relaxed" and many likened the experienced to "a mini-vacation."

Capitalizing on the theme of relaxation and vacations, I suggested that she hold a referral raffle where anyone who referred a new client that purchased a 60 minute massage ($100 value) during the next two months would receive an entry into a drawing for a 3-day trip for 2 to Miami, Florida, including the airfare and round-trip transfers.

Rhonda was a bit apprehensive at first because she thought that the costs would be expensive. So to keep travel costs down, we worked with a local travel agent who agreed to offer the hotel accommodations for free in exchange for promoting the travel agency as a sponsor on all of the promotional materials, which also included a $50 discount voucher that could be used at the travel agency when booking any vacation package of 3 days or more. The only costs Rhonda would have were the airfare from any major airport and the transfers.

Rhonda emailed all of her current clients and also sent a mailer which announced the Referral Raffle, which explained that they would receive a raffle ticket for each new referral which turned into a client. The more people they referred, the more entries they would receive.

Her clients responded positively.

At the end of the contest period, 27 of Rhonda's existing clients qualified for the raffle by referring 41 new clients. Of the 41 new clients, 8 referred 11 *additional* new clients for a total of 52 new clients who purchased a 60 minute massage for $100.00 ($5,200.00 in gross income). Rhonda's total expenses were $1,800 for the airfare, transfers, and promotional materials, netting her a cool $3,400.00 profit generated from her new clients.

Since then, Rhonda has used the Referral Raffle to incentivize her referral sources that were not her clients, such as chiropractors, physical therapists, acupuncturist, and wedding planners. Following the same process, she had a 32% increase in the amount of referrals from her non-client sources during a three-month period of her Referral Raffle.

Chapter 7

From Competition to Collaboration

Most business people view their competitors as those who are trying to lure away their clients. Open any newspaper or turn on any TV channel and you will see advertisements and commercials from everyone from car dealerships to plumbers to attorneys, each trying to outdo one another in an effort to gain new clients, spending tens of thousands of dollars in the process.

However, the smart business person sees an opportunity to generate referrals by collaborating with their competitor as can be seen in these two examples:

The "Friend of" Referral:

In New York City, there are many districts which cater towards certain industries, professions, and businesses. It is very common to see many of the same types of businesses all on the same block all competing against each other. For example, the Perfume District spans from 34th Street down to 28th Street along Broadway. Dozens of big shops and tiny kiosks sell perfumes from around the world to everyone from other store owners to the public. The competition is very fierce among the merchants as many sell the same brands and try to out price each other in the district.

Each year, rents are raised an average of 15% to 25% and in an economic downtown, a weakened dollar causes daily fluctuations in perfume prices. Adding to the mix are the big department stores like Macy's, located right at the start of the district, which compete against these smaller merchants.

But even in such a competitive environment, there is room for collaboration and referrals among competitors that result in sales for both.

Ali and Ben have both owned stores in New York City's Perfume District for over a decade. Both stores carry several of the same brands of fragrances and perfumes. Both stores are competitively priced, but Ben and Ali developed a system that not only helps their respective clients, but also both of their businesses at the same time.

Ali chose to specialize in offering a large selection of more current and trendy brands of fragrances. If a client asks Ali for a brand he doesn't carry or which is out-of-stock, he refers them to Ben, who usually has hard-to-find and some "vintage" brands no longer carried by major department stores. When one of Ben's clients wants a trendier brand, or he is out-of-stock of a perfume that he and Ali carry, he refers them to Ali.

But instead of just leaving it to chance that the client will actually go to Ben's store, Ali will call Ben and say that he's sending Mr./Ms. So-and-So to his store and tells Ben to remember to offer them the "Friend of Ali" discount (which is usually an additional 10% off their total purchase). Ali will give the person Ben's business card, on the back of which he writes "Friend of Ali" and signs it. When the client arrives at Ben's store, he/she asks for Ben who personally greets and takes care of each of them. Ben also reminds them that because they are a

"Friend of Ali," they will receive an additional 10% off their total purchase. (If Ben isn't available, one of his employees meets the client and apologizes that Ben isn't available and offers the same discount.) Ben follows the same exact process whenever he refers someone to Ali.

This same referral technique has worked well for other types of competitive retail stores which carry specific brands or specialized items. I have seen it in use all around the world, from men's shops in London to several jewelry stores in Aruba and throughout the Caribbean.

The Overflow Referral

Marty has been in the printing business for over 20 years. He recently obtained a two-year contract to do all of the printing for one of the biggest professional sports teams in his state. With the addition of this new client, his business was at full capacity. He had to hire extra help and buy extra equipment just to keep up with the demand from both the team and his existing clients.

What should be a fortuitous situation turned into a bit of a nightmare for Marty. Several of his clients experienced delays in receiving their printed materials because of the long, extended print jobs. Several customers complained about the decline in quality and great customer service they were used to receiving from Marty and his staff. Marty also seemed to change during this time. He was stressed out and started to feel that his business had begun to consume him. He was spending less time with his family, he put on weight, and his usual, cheerful demeanor became short-tempered and very abrupt.

He realized he had to do something about this and made a decision: for the next four months, he would not take on any new clients and he made the decision to let go of some of his less-profitable clients. Instead of just turning away new clients and "firing" some of the existing ones, he reached out to Phil, a friendly competitor who Marty had known for many years. Phil agreed to take on Marty's "overflow" work during this period of time and agreed to pay Marty a small percentage of fees generated. Phil also agreed to refer Marty his "overflow" work as well as those of clients who needed more specialized printing work that Marty specialized in.

If a new client was referred to Marty during this period, he spoke to both the prospect and to the referral source to explain his situation. He then asked if they would like a personal introduction to his trusted collaborator, Phil, who had the resources and would be more than happy to help them.

Marty then sent a letter to the clients he was "letting go" which explained that because of the increasing amount of work during the next four months he would not be able handle their printing requests with the same quality and attention that he previously gave. However, because of their loyalty, he would was entrusting them to his collaborator, Phil. A few days after the letters were sent, Marty called each and every one of these clients and personally thanked them for their business and offered a guarantee: if they were unsatisfied with the first job that Phil did for them, he would do the same job, free of charge. (In the end, none of the referred clients utilized Marty's guarantee).

Marty benefitted because he had the breathing-room he needed to service his major accounts and also maintained goodwill with those he referred to Phil. Phil made money and also became a referral source for Marty as he referred several specialized jobs and even collaborated with Marty on a few projects that his print shop was not equipped to handle.

Chapter 8

Let "The Cause" Become "The Because"

Most people want to give back and help and support worthy causes that are close to their hearts, their values, and ideals. Whether it's something like medical research, disaster relief, animal or pet rescue, and helping to protect and sustain the environment, people love to connect with others that share their ideals and passions. They will donate money or volunteer their time and efforts to help raise awareness or raise money for their cause. Celebrities, sports figures, and other well-known people tend to use their status in society to support certain causes. Who hasn't seen someone wearing one or more wristbands, pins, or ribbons of different colors to signify their cause? These items not only show their support of their particular causes, it also helps to raise awareness in the hopes that other people will support and believe in those particular causes as well.

More and more businesses of all types and sizes are engaging in what has generally become known as "cause marketing." Because the definition of cause marketing has evolved over the years, people tend to confuse it with corporate philanthropic efforts or social causes promoted by non-profits or charities. I think the best definition is found on causemarketingforum.com:

"Cause Marketing encompasses a wide variety of commercial activity that aligns a company or brand with a cause to generate business and societal benefits. Cause Marketing is not 'Social Marketing,' the use by nonprofit and public organizations of marketing techniques to impact societal behavior (e.g., stop smoking, don't pollute, don't use drugs, don't drive drunk) nor is it 'Corporate Philanthropy,' the giving (without expectation of direct corporate gain) of charitable financial and in-kind grants by companies or their corporate foundations."

According to the Edleman Goodpurpose 2012[6] survey:

- 76% of consumers believe that it is OK for brands to support good causes and make money at the same time.
- When quality and price are equal, the most important factor influencing brand choice is Purpose.
- 72% of consumers would recommend a brand that supports a good cause over one that doesn't.
- 71% of consumers would help a brand promote their products or services if there is a good cause behind them.
- 73% of consumers would switch brands if a different brand of similar quality supported a good cause.

---

[6] http://purpose.edelman.com.

Causes represent a great opportunity to not only be philanthropic and give-back, but to generate referrals for your business. Now I'm in no way advocating that you exploit a cause or situation only for a financial gain; in fact, the case-study and examples I'm about to reveal will illustrate how you can help others first while ultimately generating new, qualified referrals for your business.

CASE STUDY:
The Closet Clean-Out

Judy owned a local women's boutique shop which was known in her town for selling middle to high-end designer clothing. Being well-established, it had many repeat customers and mostly gained new customers through word-of-mouth. Over the years, Judy also was active in the local business community and had been a long-time member of a local woman's business group which had over 100 members.

Judy's boutique was located about ten minutes away from a big, new shopping center which featured several well-known retail stores. These bigger stores offered similar clothing that Judy sold, but at lower prices and with a larger selection.

When we began working together, Judy expressed to me that her main goal was to keep and expand her current customer base. She knew she couldn't compete against the bigger retail stores in terms of their inventory, their lower prices and most of all, their seemingly limitless advertising budget. We needed a strategy which would not only gather public attention and notoriety for Judy, but which would also generate sales in both the short-term and in the long run.

I told Judy about an international organization called Dressed For Success, which works by referral only in helping underprivileged, deserving women who are entering/reentering the workforce to find jobs. When the women have a job interview, Dressed For Success will provide them with a suit. They will work with businesses and organizations to put together donation drives where people could donate new or nearly new business suits, handbags, and accessories.

After coordinating with the local Dressed For Success representatives, Judy and I put together a donation drive with a slight twist: we would hold a week-long "closet cleanout."

Judy sent invitations to all of her existing customers who were on her mailing list and to all of the members of the women's business group, which also contained two "tickets" and a letter. The letter explained that any of the invited guests who came to the Closet Cleanout would get a 15% discount off of their total purchase which they could use anytime during the next six months, if they donated a new or nearly new garment, handbag, or accessory to Dressed for Success. If they used the second ticket to bring a friend (i.e., a new client), who also donated a garment, they would receive a 30% discount off their total order and their friend would receive a 15% discount.

We also sent out a press release to the local newspapers which announced the Closet Clean Out drive. We invited the local TV news station to come down to interview Judy and a representative of Dressed for Success on the third day of the Cleanout. On the final day, the local newspapers came down to take photos and interview some of the participants

The final results were outstanding for everyone involved!

First, the press coverage from the event became invaluable for both Judy's store and Dressed For Success. Over 1,530 donations were made by the Closet Clean Out participants. Judy added almost 180 new customers to her client list just from the event and almost 54% of these new customers made an average purchase of $300 over the next six months, even after the 15% discount was applied.

This referral strategy will allow you to create win-win situations that support causes while generating more referrals for your business. The duration of the support can be for as long or short of a time as you want.

Here are some other brief, creative examples of how others support causes while generating continuous referrals for their business:

Exchange/Discount your Services or Products for Referrals:

A veterinarian provides local pet rescue groups with deeply-discounted services to the animals in their care. Whenever someone adopts a pet from the rescue group, they provide a certificate which offers free spay/neuter services from the veterinarian.

The pet rescue group makes the referral, knowing that many of these people are first-time pet owners who reside in the community where the veterinarian has his practice. The new pet owners will need a trustworthy, reliable veterinarian and what better veterinarian to have then the one who has already treated their new pet. Many of these people will continue to use the veterinarian's services even after the free spaying/neutering and refer other pet owners to the veterinarian as well.

Using the Charity's Resources:

If you are making donations to or helping fundraise for a charity or non-profit, you can get their volunteers/employees to refer people to your business. The organization can send a mailer, an email, or other communication to their donors which feature your business as one of their "preferred partners." You could also provide the organization's volunteers/employees with a special "friends and family" discount or some other special benefit not available to the general public.

Designated Days:

When working with a non-profit or charity, you can designate a certain day of the week or month where proceeds go directly to the cause. David Rocha, Executive Director for Jewelers for Children, said in a 2010 interview with industry publication, *JCK Magazine*, "I know a jeweler who does Battery Mondays."

"Each year he has raised around $3,000 for Jewelers for Children. People specifically wait until Monday to make sure the proceeds benefit a nonprofit," says Rocha.[7]

---

[7] Holewa, P. Jewelers Embrace Cause Marketing. (2010, May) *JCK Magazine*. Retrieved from http://www.jckonline.com/article/457290-Jewelers_Embrace_Cause_Marketing.php

These are just a few of the many different ways you can have "the cause" become the "because" – the reason – for people to do business with and to refer business to you. Find a cause near and dear to your heart and help them by using one of these strategies; or create your own and share them with us on www.leadstoreferrals.com.

Chapter 9

The Big B.R.O. Event

It's not your big brother I'm talking about. It's those people with whom you do business **B**y **R**eferral **O**nly. While we all want more referrals and would prefer to do more business by referral, all too often many people mistakenly believe that offering a monetary reward such as a "finder's fee" would motivate people to generate more referrals.

It's amazing what motivates people, especially when it comes to receiving referrals. But what people would do for a slice of pizza versus a few hundred dollars is astounding.

In *The World's Best Known Marketing Secret*, (Bard Press, 1994), Dr. Ivan Misner tells the story of a real estate professional who would offer a referral fee of $100 to anyone who provided a referral that turned into a listing of a property for sale. In the six years that this technique was done, he never gave more than a dozen fees.

He decided to try a different strategy: because he lived in wine-country he grew his own grapes. He processed the grapes, then bottled and turned them into a special vintage of wine that his friends loved. He decided to make his wine available only to people who gave him qualified referrals. The result was that he gave away more **cases** of wine in the first three years than he did in referral fees. As Ivan said:

"It sometimes amazes me, even now, how something as simple as a bottle of wine can be such a powerful incentive for people to give you referrals. But the explanation is really quite simple: because it's special. A bottle of wine that can't be bought can be worth ten times what it costs to produce when traded for something as valuable as a business referral."

Taking it a step further, one of my favorite and extremely effective incentives is to have a mixer or a party or other kind of B.R.O. event. You invite only those referral partners and those clients who gave you at least 2 qualified referrals this past year (even if they didn't work out). **The goal in having this event is not to toot your own horn, but to thank and honor the people who trust you enough to refer business to you.**

A Big "By Referral Only" Event will provide an opportunity for them to interact and network with each other. Make the event fun and memorable so that people are buzzing about you. You can do a theme party such as a luau, a casino night, or a hat party (during which everyone must wear a certain kind of hat – the more novel, the more fun).

You can do a more formal event such as an awards ceremony by giving awards to those who referred business to you over time. You can create categories for the awards such as "Most Referrals Given" or "Most Valuable Partner." There can even be fun categories such as "The Most Unusual

Referral" or "Master Connector" for those who provided referrals that led to new, profitable relationships with referral sources.

While this kind of event can work almost anytime during the year, I have found that late October or early November produce optimal results as it is right before the holidays. If you're on a limited budget, don't be afraid to ask for sponsorships from Joint Venture partners or from those who would benefit from marketing to those attending. For example, a property and casualty insurance agent may ask a towing company and an auto repair shop to sponsor the event. The sponsors' logos would be printed on the signage, on any promotional and other marketing materials before, during, and after the event. You could give testimonials or special mentions to your sponsors. If doing a B.R.O. event such as a golf-outing, they can sponsor a hole or have their logo on a set of golf balls given to all participants after the event.

If you hold a fun B.R.O. event, you will be remembered for the event by everyone who attended. You want the word about your event to spread to those who didn't attend because they didn't get an invite to your By Referral Only Event. By using this "velvet rope" approach whereby only people who provided you with referrals can attend, over time, you should see a substantial increase in referrals – even from people you don't know!

CASE STUDY:

How Harry Potter Led to More Real Estate Referrals

David is a successful Real Estate Broker in a major metropolitan city. He has been one of the top producers in his field as his business has been built mostly by referral.

While other real estate agents and brokers rely on typical methods of advertising, word-of-mouth marketing and will seek referrals from their traditional sources, David is incredibly creative and proactive in staying ahead of his competition, including enlisting the "help" of Harry Potter.

In November 2002, *Harry Potter and the Chamber of Secrets,* the second of the Harry Potter films, was released worldwide. Tickets were often sold out at most theaters around the world as Harry Potter mania went global.

David decided to conduct a B.R.O. event just for those people who had referred him clients during the past year, regardless if the potential sellers or buyers went with him.

Knowing that most movie theaters were closed during certain hours of the day and were also available for rent for special functions, and seeing how Harry Potter mania was sweeping the globe, David approached a local multiplex movie theater and rented out one of their theaters during one weekday afternoon, before it would be used by the public. David purchased movie tickets to the *Harry Potter* movie, a small soft-drink and small popcorn for over 100 people.

He then sent invitations to his top 50 referral sources and invited them and a guest to attend a free, ***private screening*** of *Harry Potter and the Chamber of Secrets* on a Wednesday morning in late December.   Most of the invitees immediately took him up on his offer, rearranging their schedules and some took their kids with them since they were on Christmas break. There were a few who could not attend, so David offered their tickets to those he grouped into his next level of referral sources.

When people arrived at the movie theater, they were escorted into the theater that was showing the film by an usher. Before they went inside, David and staff members from the movie theater were giving out the popcorn and soft-drinks.

Right before the movie started, instead of the usual coming attractions being shown, David had prepared a special two-minute video which showed him in various photos with most of the attendees. The audience was delighted to see themselves on "the silver screen" and the video ended with David just saying five simple words: "Thank You for Your Referrals!"

YOUR NEXT STEPS:

1. What kind of By Referral Only incentive or event could you offer to your referral partners, clients/customers/patients? The more creative/exclusive the incentive or event, the more desire your will create for it, resulting in more qualified referrals.

2. Plan a B.R.O. Event within the next six to nine months. Decide if you want it to be a "fun" event or a more formal event. Once you decide the type of event, print up and give out "tickets" with an invitation to those who have given you at least two qualified referrals in the past year. Remember these referrals need to be people who need, want, or desire your products/services, not just information seekers or non-qualified individuals.

3. Resist the temptation to allow your friends who never referred you any business to attend. The goal of the event is for you to thank those who put their faith and trust in you by providing two qualified referrals to you.

> 4. Follow up with each of the attendees by thanking them for attending your B.R.O. event and remain in contact with them throughout the year. You may want to send a reminder or two about qualifying to attend the next B.R.O. event that you will hold in the future in order to encourage them to continue providing qualified referrals.

Chapter 10

Recognition Referrals

There are many people who are self-employed entrepreneurs and those who work for larger companies that rarely, if ever, get recognition for their efforts. There are clients who may love your services or products, but who aren't actively referring potential business to you.

People love to be recognized and appreciated for their efforts and achievements. Sometimes the very simple act of recognition can lead to more referrals for your business. When combined, the human desire to be recognized and the ability to recognize someone for their contributions and achievements can be used to generate referrals for your business.

The Who's Who Referral:

In 1849, British Publisher A & C Black created the first *Who's Who* directory which included the names (and later, biographical information) about the most prominent people in British society. Once someone was included in *Who's Who*, they were in it for life; so it is considered to be one of the most prestigious awards a citizen of the UK can achieve. While *Who's Who* has spawned thousands of imitators (all called *Who's Who)* in a variety of different fields/areas, people still love to be included and recognized for things that they have done.

Taking a cue from *Who's Who*, Jerry, a publisher of a community newspaper, decided to create a version of a *Who's Who* directory that featured local businesspeople along with their photos and a brief biography which highlighted their education, career achievements, associations that they belonged to, and their business information.

In 2002, Jerry published his first edition of the local *Who's Who*. What originally started out as a way to recognize and honor his top 25 clients transformed into a prestigious community honor, publication, and event looked forward to by members of the business community.

In starting his *Who's* Who, Jerry wrote a personal letter to all 25 honorees which announced their inclusion in the publication. Unlike other *Who's Who* publications which require the purchase of a book or to pay a fee for inclusion, Jerry provided a copy for free to each nominee who accepted his offer. As a bonus, he also provided a plaque commemorating their inclusion and a certificate which provided a 50% discount off of any new advertisement in his newspaper or affiliated publication which could be used within the following year. Finally, each nominee was honored at a special breakfast and given five complimentary tickets to give to employees, associates, or family members. Attending the breakfast were local political officials and community and business leaders.

The response to the first *Who's Who* was outstanding. Almost all of the 25 honorees purchased additional copies of the book to give to family, friends, and clients. Many listed their honor on their websites and in other promotional materials. They each used their discount over the course of the next year and 14 of the honorees even increased the amount of advertising they did in Jerry's community newspaper and his other publications.

When we began to work together in 2003, I suggested that Jerry use his *Who's Who* as a vehicle to lead to more referrals to his business.

Here's what we did:

- We created a system where Jerry would again include the previous year's honorees, but this time he asked each of them to nominate (i.e., refer) up to three other local business people that they knew, liked, trusted, and respected for inclusion in his *Who's Who*. For each nominee, the person had to give

reasons (i.e. an endorsement or a testimonial) as to why the person should be included.
- After sorting through all of the responses (and some duplicates), an additional 35 people were chosen to be included in the 2003 edition.
- Each of the nominees was notified of their nomination by a letter that contained the name of the person who nominated them and also contained an excerpt of the testimonial.
- If they accepted their nomination, one of Jerry's staff members contacted the honoree to write an full-page interview which was included in a special section of the *Who's' Who* called "2003 Inductees."
- Regardless if they accepted the honor to be included or not, each referral also received a certificate for

a 50% discount on a new advertisement. (All 35 did accept).

- Like the year before, Jerry held his annual breakfast, gave out plaques and copies of the book to the honorees, many of whom purchased extra copies.

The results:

- Jerry gained 22 new advertisers from the 35 honorees, valued in excess of $300,000 in annual revenue.
- At least 12 of the 35 new honorees referred at least two new clients to Jerry over the course of the next 12 months.
- Jerry created an additional revenue stream from the purchases of the additional copies of the *Who's Who*.

Jerry has successfully repeated the process each year for the past 10 years and will only consider new inductees if they are referred to him by past honorees, clients, and business leaders. Through his *Who's Who,* he was able to get referrals of new advertisers from his current advertisers and the business community.

Sardi's Approach

Sardi's is a world-renown restaurant in the Theater District in New York City. The restaurant is famous for the caricatures of Broadway stars that adorn its walls. Its original owner, Vincent Sardi, used these caricatures as a way to attract customers and commissioned a Russian immigrant, Alex Gard, to draw them and continued to do so until his death in 1948. Gard and Sardi agreed that as payment, Gard would eat one meal per day at Sardi's.

Stars and their fans flocked to Sardi's to catch a glimpse of the portraits. As a result, Sardi's became a bona fide New York City institution and was even the birthplace of the Tony Awards.

Perhaps you have clients who have been loyal to your business throughout the years; maybe you have advocates for your business who often refer you business. You can take the Sardi's approach of recognizing key clients and referral partners by recognizing them. While you don't need to paint a picture of them to adorn your walls, something as simple as recognizing or spotlighting your referral sources on your website, in your newsletters, or giving them an award can produce wonders.

The Local Celebrity

Pamela has worked in the restaurant industry for many years. When she opened her local bistro, she decided to take a cue from Sardi's and adorn her walls with the caricatures of local celebrities: not just business and community leaders, but also the "regulars" at her restaurant. She also named several dishes after some of the people who she had developed long-lasting, deep relationships with. The result was that people flocked to her restaurant to see who was on "the list." Every time a new portrait was revealed, the subject and their family and friends (and the local press) covered the unveiling. Others who were included always proudly referred their friends and family members to the restaurant.

You don't need to have a restaurant to do this. A simple message board or bulletin board at your business can work wonders. A simple expression that says "We'd like to thank the following individuals for their referrals" can lead to more referrals. People want to be seen/recognized. It makes them feel great and will make your business feel great too.

Pets Produce Referrals Too!

Theresa and Robert are veterinarians who have a state-of-the art practice in New York City. Their waiting room is filled with video monitors that show pictures of the staff members with a brief biography of each. They also show pictures of their team "in action" as well as many of their pet patients. When a pet comes in as a new patient, a photograph is taken and included in the electronic medical records.

With permission of the owner, the pet's name and photo is also shown on the video monitors of the waiting room that says "welcome to our new patient." They also include the pet's photo on their practice's Facebook page for all to see. Many pet owners then tag themselves on their pet's photo so it shows up on their Facebook Timeline. The result is that something as simple as this, at virtually no cost, and has produced new patients for their practice because it shows that Theresa, Robert, and their team take pride and great care of every pet that walks through the door.

Speaking from my own experience, when my dog Jack, a long-time patient of theirs, passed away, they used his photo as their Facebook profile photo with a note expressing their deepest condolences. This very simple gesture has caused me to refer more pet owners to their practice, despite the fact that I personally know at least 5 other veterinarians with whom I have a professional, business relationship with.

Chapter 11

The Gateway to Referrals

All too often, when we are looking to work with "bigger" organizations or companies, we tend to focus our efforts in meeting the "person in charge" of making decisions to buy our product or service. Or we will ask for an introduction to the person in a business that we believe to have the most influence. In our minds, that's usually the owner or in much bigger big companies, may be the head of a department, an administrator or director.

But what most people either forget or don't recognize is one person they really need to meet is the gatekeeper: the secretary, the assistant, the receptionist. This is a person who has relationships and influence with people such as vendors, suppliers, clients, the mailman, the delivery person as well as a host of service providers.

In our fast-paced world, many managers, directors, and owners of bigger companies may know the names of the businesses that provide their office supplies, or the water cooler and the payroll provider, but they don't necessarily know who the contacts are: the account manager, the sales person, the delivery person. Years ago, when business was "simpler," that may have been the case, but today it's usually the gatekeeper whose responsibilities usually include working with these people at one level or another.

Many sales training courses will advise you and will provide you with techniques to go around the gatekeeper to get to "the person in charge." These techniques completely ignore the fact that the gatekeeper is a person – a very important person – in the organization. I'd like to challenge that old-fashioned notion because in today's world, the gatekeeper can be a wealth of information and holds much influence. They can be incredible connectors of people, more so than the "higher ups."

Most gatekeepers know more than you do about the company, including the habits and schedules of the employees and management. They usually have a good understanding of the company's culture. They can tell you with whom they are currently doing business and the company's overall satisfaction level. Because the gatekeeper can be an integral ally due to their access to information and resources, you must include them in your networking efforts as they are someone with whom a relationship is cultivated.

From the company's perspective, the gatekeeper has an idea of how well service providers perform. They know when the delivery is late; they know the level of customer service that the company is receiving from their suppliers. They have some degree of influence over the "higher ups" at the company. Sometimes, based on their recommendations, a person may get the interview or a company may get the account.

When you are networking and prospecting, ask for an introduction to both the decision maker and also to the gatekeeper. You may say something like "I'd like to be introduced to Shelly Walker, the VP at Advantages Advertising or her assistant." While someone may not know Shelly personally, they may know another person who does work at Advantages Advertising who could introduce you to Shelly or to the gatekeeper. Or maybe they know someone at Mega Marketing who would also be a good prospect for you.

Knowing all of this, if you really want to stand out from the crowd and generate referrals for your business, here's something I have used over the years, and coached my clients to do the same, that a very extremely small minority of business people truly understand and do: **Do something for the gatekeeper!** Take them to lunch. Send them a thank-you note or flower. Make them feel appreciated. They put up with so much (both inside of their businesses and outside). For some, it's a thankless job, but it's one that wields a lot of power. Once you cultivate and build a relationship with these folks, you can have the "keys to the kingdom" practically given to you.

Jay's Gateway to Building an Empire:

Jay owns a court reporting service. Before a case goes to trial, lawyers will have a chance to question the opposing parties during what is known as a deposition, commonly referred to as an EBT (Examination Before Trial). Attorneys usually hire a private court reporting service, like Jay's, to take down the testimony of the parties involved at an EBT. The attorney usually has their paralegal, administrative assistant, or secretary make the arrangements with the other law firms involved and the court reporter.

It is common practice for law firms of all sizes to do business with more than just one court reporting service; so the competition between court reporters to become one of the "preferred providers" is intense. (Sometimes, an EBT will have two court reporters in attendance from two different companies because each attorney has their own preferred court reporters).

Although Jay's company had been established for more than 40 years and is well known in its city, he knew that to remain competitive he had maintain and increase his business by booking more EBTs with his current clients and, more importantly, he needed them to refer other law firms to do the same. Knowing that the administrative assistants and paralegals were the gatekeepers to the attorneys who would hire his company, he decided to do something special for them: each year, he has a holiday "meet and greet" party just for them -- no lawyers allowed!

Jay holds the party in a very trendy restaurant which he takes over for the entire night. Prior to the party, he sends invitations to the staff members of his clients, inviting them to the party, along with a gift for the entire support staff, such as a gift basket containing candy, popcorn, or other assorted goodies. (He also sends thank-you notes and gifts to the attorneys, but the support staff always gets bigger and better gifts.)

At the party, Jay and his staff make sure to meet and talk to every guest. They enjoy a nice dinner together and entertainment. (It's not uncommon for his parties to have about 200 or more attendees.) After the party, he sends a signed note to each and every attendee, thanking them for coming. The note also contains a soft but direct request that they remember to book their next EBT with his company and to refer their friends who work in the legal field who need court reporting services.

Because Jay and his staff cultivated relationships with the support staff members of some of the biggest and smallest law firms, Jay has grown his business exponentially over the years to become one of the "Top 3" court reporting services in his area. This success has helped him to create a network of court reporters across the United States.

Remember, the gatekeeper's "gate" swings both ways. It can provide an entryway to grow your business or an exit from future sales and referrals. Always remember to treat the gatekeeper with respect and dignity because you just don't know who they know.

YOUR NEXT STEPS

1. Identify the gatekeepers that you know by name at certain companies or organizations. Also identify those whom you don't know well enough and need to build relationships with.

2. When calling or communicating with them, make it a point to find out their birthday or their anniversary date (be it their marriage or even their anniversary at their job). Send them a card or a small gift, such as flowers or a gift card. (Sendoutcards.com is great for doing this!) More often than not, none of your competitors have ever done this – maybe their boss never did it either! They will remember you, take your phone call, and provide you with the information that you need.

> 3. Always be kind and courteous to them. If their company does business with yours, ask them for honest feedback as to the quality and services your company has provided. If it's satisfactory, ask them if they would be willing to refer others they deal with at other businesses to you. Because "birds of a feather flock together," they typically will talk to gatekeepers at other organizations and will share information which could result in a referral to you.

Chapter 12

The Referral Clinic

Adam is an attorney who had started his own practice about two years prior to meeting me. Fresh out of law school, he got a job working for a mid-sized law firm that had several practice areas ranging from real estate and employment law to family law. Adam had worked in each of these practice areas for the four years he was with the firm and eventually, he decided to go out on his own.

When Adam opened his own office, he marketed himself as a general practitioner; but by the time we met, he wanted to focus more on family law. He needed a way to generate referrals while at the same time, educating others about his transition into a family law practice.

As I got to know Adam, I discovered he loved coffee. On some occasions, he met clients at local coffee shops. There was a particular café near his home that he would stop at before driving the 10 miles to his office. Being a solo-practitioner, he had to get his own coffee; so each afternoon around 2 pm, he would take time out for a latte at the Starbucks near his office where he became known as a "regular" and where some of the other "regulars" would ask Adam for some basic legal advice, which he was happy to give.

I suggested that Adam use his coffee time to generate new business referrals in conjunction with generating some positive word-of-mouth marketing. We created a referral generator called the "coffee clinic" hosted at the Starbucks he frequented near his office. Here's what we did:

Every Wednesday from 2 to 3 pm, for a period of four weeks, Adam would be at the Starbucks. For that hour, he would offer free legal advice to anyone who had a question. He arranged with the store manager to put up a sign that offered free legal advice in the "coffee clinic" which was sponsored by Adam's law office. Participants would receive a free cup of coffee (regular, not the lattes or other creations) or tea which Adam paid for.

If a person had an issue that went beyond Adam's expertise, he would refer them to colleagues that focused in those areas. If a person wanted to meet privately with Adam, they would either continue the meeting at his office or he would schedule a consultation with them at a later time.

At the end of the four weeks, Adam had a total of 42 people who participated in the "coffee clinic," 11 of whom became paying clients. From those 11 clients, he received 7 new client referrals within the next three to six months. But what Adam didn't expect were the 21 residual referrals over the next six to ten months from a) those who attended the "coffee clinic" and never became his client and, b) some of the staff members and other regulars at Starbucks who got to really know Adam and what he did for a living.

YOUR NEXT STEPS:

1. Decide what kind of "clinic" you can offer to your community that will give you the opportunity to showcase your expertise and, at the same time, help others to resolve problems.

2. Identify places where your potential referral sources frequent or where your potential clients are. This might be a coffee shop, a restaurant, or community center.

3. Collaborate with other professionals who draw from similar client bases. You may want to offer a special clinic for your clients which showcase the expertise of one of your colleagues as a "guest" presenter. They can reciprocate by doing the same for you with their clients.

Chapter 13

The Manilow Method

What do business referrals and Barry Manilow have in common?

Before I reveal the answer, we need to address a common misconception made by businesses people when it comes to referrals.

Most people have learned to network and build relationships with people that are in related professions, who are not direct competitors, and who share similar types of clients or resources. For example, real estate agents typically will work with and refer business to mortgage lenders, home inspectors, real estate attorneys, electricians, plumbers, and general contractors. A real estate agent's clients typically will use one or more of these professionals' services before, during, and after the purchase of a home.

But often there are times when many other professionals that we know in unrelated fields are typically overlooked because they are not-so-obvious sources. A financial advisor's "traditional" referral sources would usually include an accountant, a banker, and an estate planning attorney.

Unbeknownst to most people, it should also include the dance school owner, the landscaper, the day spa owner, and the dry cleaner. These professions not only cater to the clientele that are part of the financial advisor's target demographic, they deal with these people on a more continuous basis than the financial advisor's "traditional" referral sources' professions of an accountant or estate-planning attorney.

Now back to the original question: What do business referrals and Barry Manilow have in common?

First an explanation is in order. The question came to me after I read the opening paragraph in an article called "New Era of Vegas Acts: Stars Who Aren't Just Has-Beens" published on April 4, 2008 in *USA Today*. The article said:

"Since 2005, Barry Manilow has set up

camp for extended runs at the Las Vegas Hilton, where he has drawn crowds for months on end. How does he do it? 'Taxi drivers' word of mouth,' Manilow quips. Actually, he's not kidding. Before launching his Manilow: Music and Passion show, the crooner put on a free performance for hotel employees and ...cabbies. No fool he."

When thinking of an international superstar performer/musician/singer/songwriter, one normally wouldn't expect taxi drivers and hotel workers to be referral sources -- but they are! They and other no-so-obvious people and professions can be great referral sources for your business as well.

Manilow knew that tourists almost always ask taxi drivers and hotel workers for recommendations for shows, restaurants, and other places of interests, especially when they don't know the area well. He identified them as referral sources that could drive the business to him (literally and figuratively).

More importantly, Manilow also knew that if he wanted people to refer others to see his show, he needed to convince the sources that it was worth seeing; so he provided free performances so that those who would be making the referrals could do it from first-hand experience. In the end, most of Manilow's Las Vegas shows were consistently sold out for seven years.

Remember, referrals can come by taxi, or boat, or plane, or Internet, and of course by people. **The question is, what will you do to drive them to your business?**

YOUR NEXT STEPS:

1. Stop and think about the not-so-obvious referral sources and begin your plan of action to reach out to them. Who are they? Who deals with them on a regular basis? How can you cultivate a relationship with these people that will lead to more referrals for their business as well as yours? What kind of experiences can you provide for them that will encourage them to refer you?

2. Identify two related networks that your business belongs to and interacts with referral sources. While most people will concentrate or recognize only one network, think of this approach as focusing on a "major and minor" subject, like a college student would. For example, an IT consultant may belong to a technology network whose members could include software developers, web designers, and social media consultants. They could also belong to a business-to-business network where they would interact with people who sell office machines, office equipment, payroll services, bottled water/coffee services, and telephone services.

3. Once you have identified your networks, develop deeper relationships by meeting with the members one-to-one. Find common ground in terms of the type of clients you both share and seek ways to collaborate with each other to attract and refer those clients to one another.

4. Then identify other professions who may deal with your target market on a more frequent basis. If you don't know anyone in these professionals, ask for introductions through your various networks, current clients, your family members, and friends. Once you identify these professions and secure an introduction, offer to provide a "sample" of your products or services to their clients on a trial basis for free or at a significantly reduced rate. The goal isn't to make a fortune on these referrals, but to set the stage to generate more initial referrals and then later, 2nd, 3rd and 4th generation referrals (and then some) from these people.

5. Create an Add-On Opportunity. An Add-On Opportunity is a chance for your prospects, current clients, and past clients to purchase your product/services bundled with those of one of your referral partners. You do this by focusing on working with professions that share similar client bases.

For example, if you are a carpet cleaning company, you may want to partner with a person who sells air purification systems to offer a discount on the units. If you are a photographer, you may want to partner with a local restaurant to offer free photographs taken of guests, one or two nights a week, offering the photos for sale in a nice frame afterwards. (The frame will have your contact information on the reverse side.)

By offering an add-on opportunity to your original product, your referral partner can pay you a percentage of their fee. If you are not comfortable splitting fees (or if your profession prevents you from splitting fees or offering referral/finder fees), your referral partner can give you their product or service for free in exchange for access to your new customer's information. That way, they may separately market their products/services to them at a later time.

Chapter 14

Your Hidden Referral Partners

Every business has many hidden referral partners. Most of them are so well "disguised" that most of us do not know they are even there. But once we discover them, we come to learn that these people belong to and have access to many different networks, communities, and potential referrals for our businesses; the problem is that *they don't even know it.*

So who are these hidden referral partners that we encounter on such a routine basis, yet remain invisible?

Vendors and Suppliers: Ours as well those of as our clients

Whether it is the local automotive repair shop or a Madison Avenue advertising agency, almost every type of business has a vendors or suppliers who either provide products or services to you or sell them on your behalf. On some level, vendors and suppliers want to help to make your business a success so that you can continue being their client and they can continue to make money with you. But all too often, our vendors and suppliers only look at you as their client/customer. In order to lead them into generating referrals for your business, you need to shift their focus into realizing that you're more than just their client.

Likewise, many of our clients work with various professionals that can be great referral sources for us, just as we can be for them. The challenge for most people is two-fold: 1) first identifying who these vendors and suppliers are, and 2) getting our clients to introduce us to them.

Getting Picture-Perfect Referrals

One of my favorite examples of a referral technique that overcomes the challenge of identifying vendors and suppliers who can be mutual referral sources and getting the introduction to them comes from Salvatore Cincotta, a photographer in St. Louis, Missouri. He writes a blog, www.behindtheshutter.com, where he shares his experiences and offers great tips to other photographers. In one of his blog posts,[8] he indicated that over the years, his business and its referral sources have changed dramatically. When he first opened his studio, 60% of his business came from bridal shows. For his 2013 wedding bookings, 45% came from client referrals, 33% from advertising and 22% from vendors such as catering halls, florists, make-up artists, etc.

---

[8] This technique is based on his post at https://www.behindtheshutter.com/getting-vendor-referrals

Wanting to increase his number of vendor referrals, Salvatore decided to focus on using a technique that he used to use years before during his slow seasons to generate more vendor referrals, but he added a more efficient, modern twist to it. Here's exactly what he did:

1. Years ago, he would go through all of his various wedding photos he took during the entire year and select the best ones that showcase some of the various vendors' items, products, or location. For example, he would select the best photos showing flowers from a certain florist, and would print up a 16x24 photo which he would mail to the florist. He found this to be effective, but incredibly time-consuming.

2. These days, when a bride and groom come to look at their photos after their wedding, he would go through the digital photos and see which ones would showcase some of their various vendor's items, products, or location. After they leave, he then takes the best photos from their wedding that showcases the reception hall and close-up shots for the make-up artist, flowers from

the florist, etc. and keeps them in separate directories. (NOTE: His contract with clients specifies that he owns the copyrights to the photos, so he has the ability to send it to magazines, vendors, etc.)

3. Once the photos are selected, each photo has his logo placed on it. He then burns them to a branded DVD and sends them to each of the vendors involved in that wedding and sends it to them with a letter printed on linen paper, which is inserted into the DVD. The letter thanks the individual vendor for their work and gives permission for them to use the photos in *their* marketing materials and websites **provided that his logo remains and that he is given credit for the photo.**

Salvatore says, "This process takes me maybe 30 minutes per wedding, and now as a result, our images are all over St. Louis, on every major vendors' website, and every vendor **LOVES** us for getting them images so quickly."

He recommends to his fellow photographers: "Find a process that works for you and your business to get images for your vendors in a reasonable amount of time after the event to create a huge referral network that will generate more business for you then you could ever imagine!"

In this example, Salvatore has created exceptional value to his client's vendors/suppliers. He provides them with free, professional photographs branded with his logo that they can use to market their respective businesses. Some of these vendors may have already worked with him in the past and new ones are easily "introduced" to Salvatore through the mutual clients.

Even if you are not in the photography business, here are some other examples of uncovering hidden referral partnerships that have been used by other professionals:

"Ambition gets your foot in the door, consistency keeps you there" -- Unknown

Most financial advisors seek referral relationships with CPAs. In fact, *The Wall Street Journal* reported that, according to a recent survey by *Financial Advisor Magazine*[9] 82% of financial advisors view accountants as great referral sources. But it's rare that most financial advisors get their foot in the door with accountants; rather the door is often slammed in their face because most of these advisors come on too strong, pushing and selling products – an instant turn-off to the accountant.

Frank is one of the rare financial advisors who gets in front of an average of 7 new accountants per year and generates hundreds of new referrals. He does this in a manner that adds value to each accountant's practice.

---

[9] How To Woo an Accountant. Retrieved on October 2, 2012 from http://blogs.wsj.com/wealth-manager/2011/11/22/how-to-woo-an-accountant/

First, he obtains his clients' accountant's information when they begin to work together. After the initial meeting, Frank sends an introduction letter to the accountant indicating that he is working with their mutual client and he follows-up with an introductory telephone call. Not once will he ever mention his services/products unless he is specifically asked by the accountant.

In the initial contact, he secures permission to some information that the accountant can use in their practices, such as how new tax laws may affect their mutual clients' investments or lists of various end-of-year resources that they can use.

Each quarter, Frank sends a portfolio summary, which also contains specific information to make the account's job easier. For example, Frank provides the cost-basis of each investment as well as the capital gains and losses the client incurred. This is incredibly helpful because the accountant needs this information when preparing tax returns and, although easily available to Frank, it usually takes the accountant a lot of time to obtain. Frank also adds value by holding twice-a-year, private meeting with his clients and their accountants regarding potential tax issues.

Finally, putting a spin on the Big B.R.O. Event technique described earlier in this book, Frank has a summer cookout for the accountants and their spouses/partners of his top 10 clients as well as the new accounts he has met in the past year through his new clients.

This is not an event for Frank to toot his own horn; instead it is to thank the accountants for the great work that they have done in the past year with his mutual clients. It also serves as a bit of an informal networking event amongst the accountants. Frank then follows-up with each attendee and continues to build and solidify the relationships. Once the relationship is in place, Frank will refer the new clients to them if one of his does not have or is unhappy with their current accountant.

Using this approach, Frank usually adds an average of seven new accountants as referral sources each year and it has led to hundreds of new, qualified client referrals from these accountants.

When You're The Client: How to Get Suppliers & Vendors to Refer Business To You

Think about the amount of money you spend, both personally and professionally with vendors and suppliers. How much money have you spent in the past year with your dentist? Your drycleaner? How much have you paid the company that cleans your office? What about the company you purchase your office supplies from? Your landscaper or insurance agent?

Chances are you have spent several thousands of dollars with these people over the course of your years with them.

Think about how large their client base is. The longer they are in business chances are the larger their client base is. Do you think that some of their clients could use your products or services? (Hint: you should be saying yes at this point.)

Then think about how much money have they spent on you in the past year? How many referrals have they given you in the past year?

For the majority of people, chances are the answer is **ZERO!**

Why?

It's usually due to the fact that they only know you or view you as their client/customer/patient. You have to change their perspective and let them know that you're *more than just their client!*

One insurance agent did just that… and became a billionaire!

Walter's story:

The late, great author and sales trainer Zig Ziglar often wrote and spoke about his friend Walter Hailey. Hailey was one of the most successful insurance agents in the world – so successful that he ended up buying the insurance company that he worked for, Lone Star Life Insurance. Hailey later went on to develop several other businesses, including a wholesale food insurance company which he sold to Kmart in 1973, and developed several other companies which he took public.

Hailey created a very simple system which he called NEER™ which stands for Naturally Existing Economic Relationships. From 1987 until his death in 2003, he taught this system to thousands of business people from around the world who paid an average of $1,000.00 per person to attend his "Boot Kamps" held at his ranch in Central Texas. He even wrote a book called *Breaking the NO Barrier* (Triamid Press, 1992).

The NEER™ system is based on the saying "follow-the-money." Hailey realized that once a person or business becomes the client of another, the provider of the service/product has an economic interest in keeping and making the customer happy.

Hailey decided to leverage those relationships by contacting and visiting those people with whom he was the client and would ask them for referrals for his business, while at the same time, showing the value to both his business and theirs. More often than not, he would get referrals from his vendors because they had a stake in Walter's success. The more successful that he became, the stronger the relationship became between him and his company and their businesses. Hailey also realized that his competitors were not even going to their vendors/suppliers, thus giving his business even more leverage.

Regardless of your business or its size, there are several ways to help shift their view of you as being "just a client" to being a referral partner. Here are two case studies:

The Dentist and the Daycare Center

Beverly is a dentist who opened her own practice about four years before we met. She is married to a high school principal and, at the time, their young daughter was in daycare for the last few years. Beverly wanted to increase the number of families as patients to her practice. I asked if her daughter enjoyed the daycare center and Beverly said that she loved it. I suggested that she look towards establishing a relationship with Daisy, the owner of the daycare center, in order to lead to more family patient referrals.

I asked Beverly if she ever told Daisy about how much her daughter loved going to daycare each day. When she said that she hadn't, I suggested that she should use the opportunity to speak to Daisy when the monthly daycare bill came in the mail. I suggested rather than just mailing a check, Beverly should hand-deliver it to Daisy and use this moment to express her gratitude for running such a great daycare center and to tell of her daughter's delight.

She took my advice. She told Daisy how much her daughter looks forward to coming to daycare each day and how she and her husband feel very comfortable in having her there and in recommending the daycare center to other parents. As an expression of her gratitude, and knowing that people usually need to experience her services before she can ask for referrals, she offered Daisy and her immediate family a complimentary dental visit.

After Daisy and her family accepted the offer and had a great experience with Beverly, Daisy began to tell others she knew as well as the parents of the children in her daycare center about Beverly's dental practice.

In the first year, Daisy referred eight new families to Beverly, some of whom were here current clients, while others were friends and former clients that Daisy kept in touch with. That same year, Beverly also referred six new parents with children who needed daycare to Daisy. This led to both women starting a professional relationship and personal friendship. Beverly now has some of Daisy's marketing materials in her waiting room so that her patients could read about her practice.

You "Auto" Know Hank

Hank was a client of mine who owns a local auto repair shop. He gets his parts from several local auto parts distributors. Because the parts are usually needed same-day, the distributors have employees who personally deliver the parts that are ordered by the repair shops. Most of the distributors' employees use their own cars, which frequently need servicing from all of the extra driving and wear-and-tear. I suggested that Hank tap into this market.

We came up with a very simple way to generate more referrals: Using Sendoutcards.com, we designed a custom greeting card that was sent to each of the distributors which thanked them for reaching "preferred vendor" status. The card also offered a special "thank you" to them and their employees: a 50% discount on an oil change and service packages during the next three months. In the three months that followed, Hank had a 21% increase in business just from sending out the greeting cards.

A few months later, we repeated this strategy, but this time, we targeted local pizza shops and Chinese restaurants within a 5 mile radius of Hank's shop that he and his staff would frequently order lunch or dinner from and have delivered. Because the employees of these restaurants often use their own personal vehicles to deliver the meals, we created a card which thanked these restaurants for "delivering" great food and value. The same

50% discount offer given to the parts distributors and their employees was also made.

In the three months that followed, Hank had an 18 % increase in sales just from the pizza and Chinese restaurants. This led Hank to develop additional advertising, co-marketing and referral opportunities with several of the restaurants which tapped into their regular customer base.

Remember that your vendors and suppliers have a treasure trove of potential referrals for your business, *if* they know about you. You need to engage them and help them to see that you're more than just their client. Continuously educate and motivate them while adding value to their businesses and you will have a steady stream of referrals coming your way.

Chapter 15

I See, You See Referrals

"A great referral for me would be someone you know that has a high credit score," said the mortgage lender.

"I'd like to be introduced to someone who is unhappy with their dentist," said a dentist.

"I'm looking for a business owner that wants a line of credit," said a banker.

How often have you heard phrases similar to these when someone was trying to describe their ideal type of referral? (At times, perhaps you have found yourself mentioning similar lines.) Usually, whenever I hear requests like this, I walk away from the conversation thinking to myself "I really don't know…." Or "How would I know if…."

There are a few problems with this type of referral request.

First, it assumes that other people are viewing a potential referral from your point-of-view. Because you work with your clients on a routine basis and with people in the same or similar professions, you see, hear, and know things that others who are not in your field do not. It may be easy for a mortgage lender and a financial advisor to know someone's credit score, but someone like a photographer or a contractor may not. (After all, people typically don't walk around with their credit score written on their shirts.) And yet, the photographer and general contractor may be able to make qualified referrals to that mortgage lender *if* they knew what to notice or look for.

If the mortgage lender could say, "A great referral for me would be someone you know that is employed at the same job for more than 3 years, has a family, and is renting an apartment that they are outgrowing. Chances are that their credit score is good enough for us to help them qualify to purchase a home."

The mortgage lender sees their credit score, we don't. What we do see is the family, their apartment which seems to be getting smaller as the kids get bigger, and we know the person who has the steady job.

Instead of the banker asking to meet business owners who want a line of credit, he should tell us to look for the business that has recently hired more people or which seems busier than usual, filling orders or expanding their size.

The dentist should tell us, "When you see a person with a bright, white smile, that person is an ideal referral for me because they like to take care of their teeth and care about their appearance."

Whenever you describe a potential referral, you have to tell others what they are going to see and notice -- which is not necessarily the same exact thing you will see.

The second problem is that it only tells us what the recipient wants, not what the prospect wants. After telling the source what to look for, the second step is to define a "want/need/desire or result" from the prospect's perspective. So using the example of the mortgage lender, the referral request may be framed this way:

"A great referral for me would be someone you know that is employed at the same job for more than 3 years, has a family, and is renting an apartment that they are outgrowing *(what we see)*. Chances are that their credit score is good enough for us to help them qualify to purchase a home. Once they're in that new home, the kids will have their own rooms; mom and dad will have a master suite with their own bathroom and the family can have the dog they always wanted. The kids will be playing in the backyard while the rest of the family and friends come over for a summer barbeque."*(the want/need/desire/result).*

The dentist could say:

"When you see a person with a bright, white smile, (**what we see**) that person is an ideal referral for me because they like to take care of their teeth and care about their appearance. Perhaps they want to appear to take years off their true age. Maybe they are in a profession that requires a lot of face-to-face meetings or interaction, such as an attorney or salesperson, and they want to ensure that they leave a lasting first impression." (***the want/need/desire/result***).

So whenever you are making a referral request to your contacts, make sure to always tell them what 1) they should see to identify a qualified referral, and 2) then tell what the clients usually want, from the client's perspective.

This simple, yet detailed technique will lead to getting more qualified referrals as it creates a connection between the source, the prospect, and the receiver of the referral.

YOUR NEXT STEPS:

1. Make a list of five things that potential referral sources could potentially see or notice when they may encounter a potential, qualified referral for you.

2. For each of the five, describe from the prospect's perspective their motivations, wants, needs, and desires that could trigger the opportunity to make the referral to you

3. Describe, from the prospect's point-of-view, their expected results when they finish working with you.

4. When presenting this to your contacts and sources, see if they would agree with your assessment and then ask them for feedback to fine-tune the referral request. When you do this, you are actually getting them to focus on what *they* believe they will encounter or notice in their respective networks, causing them to be more attentive to and ready for the opportunity to make a qualified referral to you.

Chapter 16

Closed Loop Referrals

All too often, businesspeople don't realize that there are often inconsistencies in the origins of their referred clients. Most people and organizations have *pre-purchase* reasons, needs, or criteria that lead someone to refer them to you.

So it's natural that we tend to believe that if clients have a great experience or if we resolve their problem or challenge, their post-purchase, positive word-of-mouth will often result in our referral sources to continuously refer new, qualified clients to us.

But there's a catch: this assumes that our clients are returning back to the referral source with positive feedback about their experiences.

But what happens when they don't?

How can you motivate you clients to provide the necessary feedback to your referral sources, which, in turn, can result in those sources providing you with a continuous stream of qualified referrals?

In 1998, Alnur Dhanani, an owner-manager of an independent, three-star hotel in the United Kingdom, found himself in that very situation which became the subject of a research study at Kingston Business School[10] and which became the basis of what I call "Closed Loop Referrals."

Alnur was seeking to increase his hotel's occupancy rates. On average, 70% of his clients were tourists – most of them from overseas. The other 30% were business travelers. Alnur believed that it was incredibly difficult to get more tourists to stay at his hotel, since he did not have as wide of a reach (or budget) to attract his ideal customers, as compared to the chain hotels.

---

[10] David Stokes, Wendy Lomax, (2002) "Taking control of word of mouth marketing: the case of an entrepreneurial hotelier," *Journal of Small Business and Enterprise Development*, Vol. 9 Issue 4, pp.349 – 357.

Alnur began working with researchers from Kingston Business School to measure the effect of word-of-mouth referrals on his hotel's bookings with tourists. They surveyed the hotel's clients during the hotel's busy season. Of the respondents, 80% were tourists. The research revealed:

- Only about 12% of his guests booked their stay directly with his hotel, while 85% of guests used a travel agent or a tour operator, since they were largely from overseas.
- 25% of them booked the hotel because of its price, location, and facilities.
- 52% said that the hotel was recommended to them; 72% of which were referred by travel agents or tour operators.
- 70% of respondents found the recommendation to be the most important or quite an important factor in choosing the hotel.
- 92% of respondents were satisfied with the hotel.

But there were some other eye-opening results:

- 53% said that they would **not** have chosen the hotel just because it was recommended to them.
- 99% said they would discuss their trip afterwards with others, of which 90% said that they would specifically talk about the hotel, but:
    - 70% said they would talk to friends and family about the hotel.
    - But only 30% were likely to talk to their travel agent – the primary source of the hotel's clients – about the hotel.

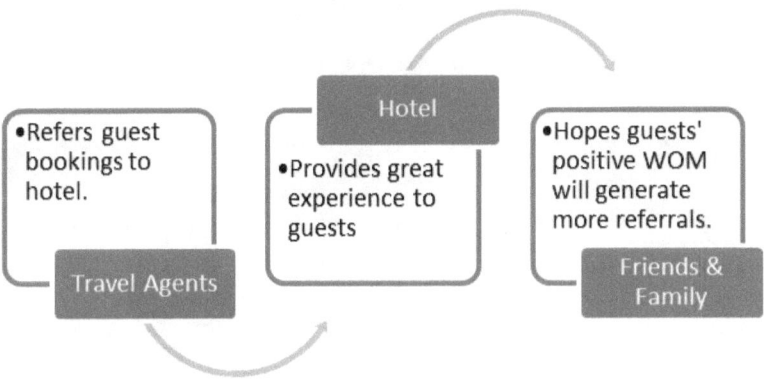

(Figure 1: The "open loop": Relies on Word-Of-Mouth).

Faced with such a disparity, Alnur realized he needed to do something in order to lead his guests back to their travel agents and tour operators – his main source of referrals -- with stories about their amazing experience at his hotel. He knew this would motivate the travel agents and tour-operators to refer more guests on a reliable, regular basis.

He developed a two-part approach which closed the open loop by creating a novel incentive program which stimulated and led both his guests and sources alike to refer more business.

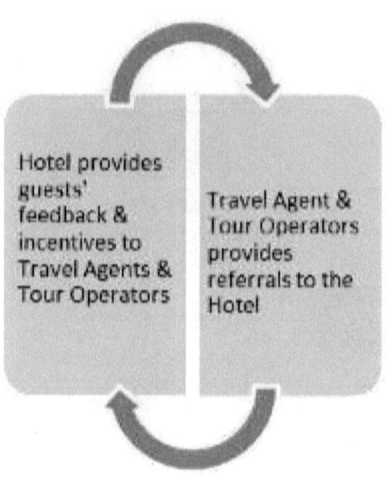

(Figure 2: Closed Loop Referral Process: Travel Agents)

Closing the First Loop: Travel Agents

1. Whenever guests filled out a comment card, a summary was sent to the travel agent that referred the guests. This step ensured that the agent received the necessary feedback about the guests' experience without leaving it up to chance that the guest would communicate with their travel agent, post-trip.

2. Travel agents who booked a certain number of times were given "reminders of England" by receiving a miniature Paddington Teddy Bear which were followed up periodically with several small jars of honey with a note from the hotel reminding the agent to "feed" the bear. Not only did this differentiate the hotel from its competitors, it provided top-of-mind awareness of the hotel and made it easier for the agents to refer their clients, all without having to pay a higher commission rate to the agents.

Realizing that personal experiences lead to the best testimonials which, in turn, influence others, travel agents, travel writers and tour operators were given complementary stays in order to experience the hotel for themselves

Closing the Second Loop: The Guests

Although the hotel had a 92% satisfaction rate, Alnur closed the second loop by providing his guests with incentives during their stay. This helped to further stimulate post-purchase, positive word-of-mouth while at the same time, transforming the guests' experience into a referral generating opportunity.

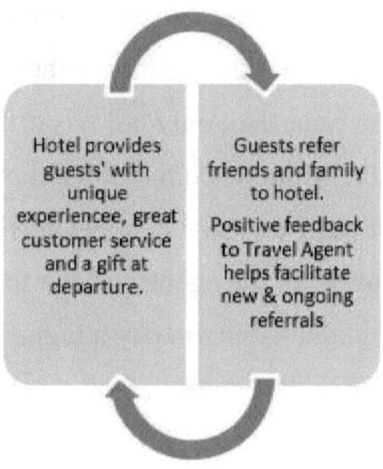

(Figure 3: Closed Loop Referral Process: Guests)

Here was his strategy:
1. Guests were also given a miniature Paddington Teddy Bear upon their departure, which reminded them of the novel aspects of the hotel.
2. Guests were given a detailed pocket map which showed the hotel's location in relation

to important tourist locations, transportation facilities and comparative costs.

3. Alnur invested in the facilities of the hotel, restoring several rooms back to their original 1860's look, complete with period furniture.

4. An "honesty bar" was placed in the lounge area where guests could help themselves to beverages and pay, on an honor system, for what they consumed.

5. Guests' complaints, normally handled by junior staff, were now handled by senior managers, whom guests had direct access to during their stay. This helped to reduce complaints and resolve situations as they occurred.

Results:

Travel agents who received the teddy bear and honey gave **three-times more referrals** than the ones who didn't.

The "honesty bar" only worked for about 30% of the entire hotel because it was in a separate VIP section; however the repeat customers and their referrals from that section were higher than the other 70% of the hotel.

Because of the "closed loop referral" strategy, occupancy rates increased substantially over the next 18 months. This is a great example of how a business can intervene, influence and transform the WOM process from a passive activity into a one that stimulates and leads to additional referrals.

Chapter 17

Now What?

> *"The path to success is to take massive, determined action."*
>
> *--Anthony Robbins*

Congratulations! You made it to this point and are probably wondering where or how to start getting your contacts that count to provide you with new, rewarding qualified referrals. You may be excited to try several strategies and techniques or you may be suffering from information overload.

My suggestion would be to start by implementing the one strategy that appeals to you most based on the type of business you have, or the size and quality of the people in your network. If you have a retail business to consumer business, and are looking to motivate your client base, techniques like The Referral Raffle or the Double-Triple Referral Reward could be a good start. If you have a business-to-business model or have many referral sources, then the techniques like The B.R.O. Event or the strategies outlined in the chapter on Recognition Referrals may be best.

The secret to making *Leads to Referrals* work for your business is to take action and start implementing what you have learned. Use this book as a guide, take notes, and keep track of what works and what isn't working for you. Read and re-read paragraphs and chapters in this book – but take action!

Take advantage of some of the additional trainings and resources found on www.leadstoreferrals.com and share your experiences with me and others on the website. Remember that in order to get more rewarding referrals, you need to continuously earn the privilege of receiving them from your sources. Their personal and professional reputation is on the line with every referral they give to you. The strategies and techniques in this book will help you to continue to build new relationships and enhance the existing ones.

No matter which techniques or strategies you employ, always remember to add continuous and exceptional value to the lives and businesses of those you serve. When you do, you will find that these things will lead to more referrals, but will make your business and your life more productive, profitable, and prosperous.

Meet Tim Houston

Tim Houston is a bestselling author, speaker, and entrepreneur. He has dedicated himself to helping businesses of all sizes to become more productive, profitable and prosperous through referral marketing, business networking and development.

Crowned "The Czar of Networking" by CBS Radio, Tim has positively impacted thousands of business people through his high-energy seminars, workshops, motivational presentations, and mentoring sessions. His first book, *The World's Worst Networker: Lessons Learned By The Best From The Absolute Worst!* (Createspace, 2011) became the #1 bestseller in seven categories in six countries on Amazon.com. He is a contributing author to *The New York Times* Best Seller List and multiple #1 Best Seller, *Masters of Sales* (Entrepreneur Press, 2007).

Tim is a graduate of Fordham University and resides in New York City.

Learn how Tim can make your business or organization more productive, profitable, and prosperous at www.tmhouston.com and get additional resources and trainings at www.leadstoreferrals.com.

Also By Tim Houston

The #1 International Bestseller!

Tim Houston and several of the world's best networkers take an uncensored look at the way some people conduct their business networking, online and offline. Their stories and experiences about these nightmares of networking will teach you how *not* to network.

**Learn more at
www.worldsworstnetworker.com**

www.ingramcontent.com/pod-product-compliance
Lightning Source LLC
Chambersburg PA
CBHW030742180526
45163CB00003B/899